FATHER TO SON

WORDS OF WISDOM

EVERY SON SHOULD CONSIDER

Eric Willis

Father to Son: Words of Wisdom Every Son Should Consider
©2018 Eric Willis

All rights reserved. No part of this book may be reproduced, scanned, or distributed in any printed or electronic form without permission. Please do not participate in or encourage piracy of copyrighted materials in violation of the author's rights.

X-Protégé Publishing
Dallas, Texas

Cover Design: The Design Factory
Graphic design, Rhonda Howard
Interior Design, Eric Willis
Robert Swan, Editor

Management: Nichelson Entertainment
1402 N. Corinth Street - Suite 125
Corinth, Texas 76208
nichelsonentertainment.com

Library of Congress Cataloging Data TXu001999677

ISBN: 978-09857631-5-2

APPLAUSE FOR FATHER TO SON

"Since my father never spent any significant time with me, I had lots of unanswered questions about life. Father to Son answers those questions and speaks in a way that will enhance every man. Explore this powerful book to discover the lessons that life may have failed to render to your soul."
— Quintine Perry, Human Resource Officer

"In my years of coaching community football, it was easy to spot the kids who lacked an engaging relationship with their father by his absence from practice and games. Fatherless kids savor every word spoken because they desire to hear the voice of a man who cares. Father to Son has the caring voice that I intend to give to each of my players."
— OMAR LANDRUM, POLICE OFFICER, FOOTBALL COACH

"Sharon and I are fully engaged parents who keep very active schedules of our own. As a touring musician, I must find creative ways to collaborate with my wife to guide our sons. We can only imagine what their lives would be like without a voice to lead them. For those who lack this guidance, Father to Son is an immensely valuable book."
—THOMAS BRAXTON - RECORDING ARTIST, SHARON BRAXTON - VOICE ACTOR

"I wish this book had been available to me when raising my son. I would have gained profound insight for helping him overcome the challenges that boys face."
—CARLA DENISE, SINGLE MOTHER

APPLAUSE FOR FATHER TO SON

As a thirty-year old man, this book says important things to me that no one in my life has ever said.
—WILLIAM DAVIS

"Eric Willis has authored a must-read treasury for anyone raising a male in today's society...Read this book and pass along the timeless wisdoms to your male children."
— Rhonda Howard, Educator

"We should never underestimate the powerful role a father plays in his children's educational achievement. Because there is a direct correlation between the missing male and academic efficiency, our young men are struggling. Father to Son provides the instruction of a caring mentor who wants his sons to succeed."
—JAMES CHARLES, ASSISTANT SUPERINTENDENT
TERREBONNE PARISH SCHOOLS

Table of Contents

Intelligence	1
Manhood	3
The Deal: Sex	6
Extended Family	10
Friends	12
Relationships	15
Codependent Relationships	17
Dating	19
It's About Love	22
Marriage	24
Fatherhood	28
Work	31
Finance	34
Responsibility	38
Business	40
Travel	42
Nutrition	44
Fitness and Health	47
Religion	50
Worship	53
Philosophy	55
Creativity	56
Leadership	58
Tenacity	60
Do It Now	62
Know God's Grace	64
Being Alone	67

OPINIONS	68
EDUCATION	69
MILITARY SERVICE	72
CIVIC RESPONSIBILITY	73
SURVEY YOUR SKILLS	74
STATIONS IN LIFE	75
FAITH	76
HONESTY	77
A BROKEN HEART	78
STRESS	79
CONFLICT	81
BE THANKFUL	83
DECEPTION	84
KEEP A JOURNAL	86
TELL YOUR STORY	87
GET SERIOUS	88
BEWARE	89
SELF-IMPROVEMENT	91
LIVE WITH LEGACY IN MIND	92
CLEAN UP ON AISLE FIVE	93
MANAGE THE BLESSING	95
CONFESS	97
BE AN EDUCATOR	98
CELEBRATE	99
MY PRAYER FOR YOU	101
EPILOGUE	103

To my wife:

Rhonda, thank you for helping me to become a better man. You are the biggest reason that my life is most fulfilling and your support has helped me accomplish goals.

To our sons, Joshua and James:

I am grateful to be your father and a guide through the first seasons of your life. I pray for your success as men, husbands and fathers.

Special thanks to my dad who largely failed at his role of being a father. It is certain that this book would not have come to fruition without your contribution to my understanding. For this, I am profoundly grateful.

Special thanks to Carolyn and her daughter Latoyce, who gifted me the journal in which I used to write the original manuscript.

Suggested approaches to reading this book:

1. **Quick Verse:** Read the first line of each entry.
2. **Topical Verse:** Choose a topic and read all entries.
3. **Continuous Verse:** Read this book from cover-to-cover.
4. **Contemplative Verse:** Focus on one section per week for an entire year.

INTRODUCTION

From the moment I became a father, I was determined to provide you with the best opportunity for a successful life. I wanted you to know that you would always be loved and I demonstrated this truth by maintaining a stable and healthy environment. In order to create a platform for your success, I had to commit to giving you the best possible education. Along with that, I wanted you to have the ability to employ wisdom and logic.

Life requires good judgement based upon deductive reasoning to make the best decisions. This is the key to producing the best results. Although every outcome may not be desirable your thinking and meditation before acting will keep you on the path to greatness.

As a father, I quickly realized that it would be impossible to tell you everything I want you to know, nor would you remember it, even if I could. With that in mind, I began to write the overflow of my thoughts on a series of topics in hopes that you will read it continually throughout your life. While my concern for you is great, it occurred to me that these thoughts, experiences and pronouncements are relevant to every son.

With this in mind, I present this book to every young man who had a sketchy relationship with his father or grew up in an unhealthy environment. I hope that you will also consider my words as they come to you sincerely, from Father to Son.

INTELLIGENCE

Read incessantly.

People will often ask how you know so much about such a wide variety of topics and will be astonished by the answer.

"I read."

1. Read books cover-to-cover.
2. Read for content. Find the section of the book that you want to understand and read it for full comprehension.
3. Read the first lines of each paragraph. Great writers often make their point in the opening statement.
4. Read backward or retrograde. In many cases, you can learn just as effectively by starting at the last chapter and work your way backward. This works well with method books because they rapidly show you the missing elements to your understanding.

Increase your ability to communicate and interact with others by learning a foreign language. This will enhance your understanding of other cultures as well as your connection to the world.

Overcome your fear of being surrounded by people who are smarter and more successful. There is a lesson everywhere you look. Observe and learn. Celebrate the advantage you gain from being in the presence of successful people.

See value in the best things people say and do. Too often, we are jealous of those who exhibit a special skill or talent and closed-minded to what they can teach us. Learn to appreciate others and see them as a valuable resource when you need help in their area of expertise.

Read a wide variety of books. Read articles about finance, business, technology, science, sociology, psychology, physics, philosophy, astronomy, medicine, history, biology, current events, and more. Continue reading for the rest of your life.

Increase your skills by studying with the greatest minds. A conversation with the right person can enhance the way you do things. A single lesson can shift your paradigm and help you bring a new concept to life. A master class will keep your skills fresh and revive your passion for the work you do.

Collect and archive resources that others tend to overlook. For instance, keep programs that identify patrons and donors who might be interested in supporting your causes. Introduce yourself when in the company of producers and promoters. Maintain those connections. Make note of interesting companies like manufacturers and fabricators. This will be useful when you need to design and build your new products.

Act on your intelligence. Your understanding gives you a distinct advantage. Use this to advance your endeavors. Your competitors may not have the insight to do so.

MANHOOD

If I get to be half the man that you are becoming, that will make me twice the man that I am now. I have a great deal of respect for you and hope you continue to make decisions that bring honor to our family. Manhood is a growth process, not just a landmark at which you will arrive. At every phase of manhood, you should experience an increase in understanding and operate with higher standards than before.

Live by your own standards. Over time, you will gather ideas and precepts that help you form your own system of thinking. Walk in your beliefs regardless of the actions of others. Standing alone is not a condition that one must suffer. It is an advantageous path that one takes to travel with less baggage and no one to slow you down.

Own up to your mistakes. This will make you a greater man than most of the men in your company. Owning up to mistakes is most often personal and internal to the extent that you are being honest with yourself.

Sometimes, owning up to mistakes calls for open confession to those who were impacted. Be courageous with your apology. Mark the moment as an accomplishment and be intentional about moving past it.

Be a man of valor. Live with a set of values upon which you stand firmly. Have a set of principles that you would defend with your life. Draw boundaries that you are committed to never cross, nor allow others to convince you to compromise. People will learn from the way you live. When they know what you stand for, there will rarely be any confrontation.

Avoid confrontations driven by your ego. Do not waste your time being in contention with others about things that have no value. Without values, your battles are a frivolous fight.

Live valiantly and let those who are petty squabble over simple things. Disengage when there is contention. Others may not use wisdom, logic or understanding at your level. This increases the chances that a conversation can turn into a brawl. Have nothing to do with this. Your manhood should not be measured by your fighting ability but by your capacity to make better decisions.

As a man, you will always be faced with challenges. When you have multiple problems, calm yourself and address them one at a time. The more problems you solve, the more confident you will become. In time, you will realize that problems do not upset you but rather motivate you to resolve issues daily.

Face the pain. Even though it is difficult to admit your faults and failures, acknowledge them and grow. Confession may be painful but it is temporary because the problem goes away. Living with your unacknowledged faults is forever.

Be the kind of man you want your sons to become. They will learn your personality, your habits and emulate you in every way they possibly can. Care for them enough to model a life of scrupulous behavior. If you refuse to uphold a standard, be honest with them about your failure so they have a fighting chance to find a better path.

Leaving your sons with a false sense of reality about the world is one of the cruelest things you can do to them. When they find their way, they will have little or no respect for you.

Be the kind of man you want your daughters to marry.
You are the standard for what they believe to be normal. You should be honored, not troubled, when they marry a guy just like you.

Be a man of peace. Practice communicating above conflict. Use calm words of wisdom. If there is no clear resolution, bid a peaceful farewell and use the nearest exit. The only physical altercation that has value is the one that lasts twelve rounds and has a multi-million-dollar purse.

Do not allow anyone to usurp your value as a man. People will often attempt to demote or diminish your value. This is a tactic used by those who are intimidated, threatened, self-absorbed, or have self-esteem issues. Do not let these encounters define the measure of your greatness. Your manhood is much more than a moment in time with injured people.

Learn to use these valuable phrases:

1. Please
2. Thank you
3. Pardon me
4. Sir
5. Ma'am
6. Excuse me
7. Continue to enhance your etiquette.

Get up and face the day.

THE DEAL: SEX

Your sex is your identity. When your mother and I announced our pregnancy, our family and friends did not ask your name. They wanted to know what sex you were. You had an identity long before you had a name. Your sex is your identity and it should be protected as carefully as any other form of identification. Do not give away your identity. Teach this principle to your children.

Having sex with your wife should be the only thing in your life that is sexy. You will be grossly distracted if you allow yourself the leisure of lust. This will also cost you time, productivity, and a great deal of money. You will lose intimacy and be on the path to losing your marriage and family.

Do not get caught up in virtual sex-oriented distractions. They are designed to manipulate you and harm you physically and emotionally.

Men are stimulated visually. Sexy contours capture our attention. Any allure for sexually explicit images can easily turn into pornography addiction and extra-marital affairs. It all starts with the eye.

Son, do not consider yourself to be in competition with your male friends for sexual conquest. Every man has his own path and values. You never know what is driving them. Some of your friends are compulsive, some may be sociopaths, and some may have predatory tendencies. You should be driven by love, respect, and adoration. These are the qualities that will help you find the person you can love for a lifetime.

Do not let your decisions be driven by sexual impulse. The lower man in you wants to celebrate his attraction to everything sexual while the higher man is ashamed of his impulsive behavior.

Son, do not measure your manhood by a quantity of sexual encounters. Upon examination, sex will have nothing to do with the measure of man you turn out to be.

When a business organization calls you "Man of the Year," it will be because of your professionalism, ethics, and significant contribution to commerce and industry.

Make up your mind to pursue the ambitions of the higher man. When you deviate from this, you will waste valuable time and literally screw yourself around.

Read books that challenge you morally. This is beneficial to protect your heart, your mind, and your family.

Do not hang with guys who celebrate debauchery or lewdness. Men engage in inappropriate conversations to be well received by other men. Let these be your acquaintances, not your inner circle of brothers.

There are multiple levels of intimacy. Holding hands is level one. Stay there for a while. Also recognize that the most intimate touch is the placing of your hand on the crown of someone's head. This is how you pronounce a blessing. Bless others with your touch.

If you are dating seriously, there are important areas that need your attention. You are looking for compatibility and longevity. Check out spending habits and debt ratio. Money issues will impact your sex life as bills pile up and spending compulsions remain unchanged. Marital failure is imminent.

The world wants pornography and eroticism to be so common that it is socially acceptable by all. In this way, you can become more easily trapped while thinking your lifestyle is normal. Avoid this without convicting others. They are simply doing what pornography and eroticism compels them to do. It is a choice, at first, then a compulsion that takes over their lives.

Your life is important. You are valuable to the people around you and an immense treasure to the family you do not yet have. That's right. You mean a great deal to your unborn (unknown) children, so live your life with this awareness.

Grow your family intentionally, not incidentally. Plan and maintain your family with your mate. Live in such a way that the fourth and fifth generations of your descendants know who you were and what you did for them. Your life is that important.

Physical connection is powerful but the emotional disconnect is painful. Since you were made for an intimate connection to an authentic relationship, it is agonizing when you are physically together but emotionally detached.

1. Your first challenge is that you choose the right person with whom to have a healthy relationship.
2. Make sure your values and goals are on the same wavelength. Although you are different people, you should have the same core values.
3. Be committed to resolve issues, offering a reasonable amount of satisfaction.
4. Desire harmony above selfishness.
5. Openly discuss your feelings. Self-talk produces anger based upon the wrong conclusions.
6. Continue to demonstrate love and respect. With time and clarity, all problems will be resolved.
7. Do everything you can to preserve your relationship.

A sinful lifestyle will separate you from real contentment. At first, your losses will be subtle until you realize that the only happiness you find is synthetic as you continually return to your vices.

Live the kind of intimate lifestyle of which you are unashamed. Your sex life should be discreet, which is not the same as a lifestyle you must hide. Do not involve yourself in activities that would ruin your marriage, career, reputation or family. No one is ever proud of their bizarre actions when they come to light.

I pray that you find the strength and courage to overcome the secret challenges in your life. This is one of the toughest battles you will ever face as a man. Victory happens when you keep your priorities before you.

EXTENDED FAMILY

In childhood, you are your father's core family but in adulthood, you become his extended family. You will eventually have a core family of your own.

Be loyal to your core family. When loyalty is your guiding principle, the family is unified.

Cherish your family. This is the entity you should be able to rely upon in times of need.

Be the most loving and reliable person in your family. Set a standard that others follow.

Be respectful of your parents and elders. Never be disrespectful. This is a values-driven disposition. If your values are higher than your elders, you must remove yourself from their company to avoid being disrespectful.

Learn to forgive. This is a commitment one must make to himself. You are letting the other person off the hook and intentionally allowing them to swim away.

Forgiving is advisable but forgetting is discretionary. In many cases, it may be completely unwise to forget past circumstances, as there are valuable lessons to retain. Remembering makes it possible to avoid decisions that lead to poor results with the same people.

True forgiveness comes after confession. It is very difficult to forgive people for things they refuse to admit they did wrong. In this case, it is plausible to withhold forgiveness in hopes that the shame will produce enough remorse that they apologize.

Sometimes you must make the difficult decision to let people go. This is especially tough when it involves a family member but you must set clear boundaries for yourself and others. You are acting out of self-preservation, not anger or malice. Life is a long-distance race. You must preserve your endurance.

Your primary purpose is to build and maintain a healthy core-family.

Your secondary goal should be to contribute love to your extended family. Love is emotional, not financial.

It is not your responsibility to be a hero or a savior. When you decide not to bail out an extended family member, you will often find that the sweet, needy person swiftly becomes someone who insults you for being cruel to them. (They go from victim to victimizer).

Be a man of reconciliation. Restore family whenever it is possible. Be the person that brings family together to resolve conflict with gentleness.

Pray for your extended family members and support them with love. We often fail them because we forget them in our prayers. Pray for their success and growth and their safety.

FRIENDS

Examine yourself. You need to know your strengths and weaknesses so that you pair yourself with those who enhance you. Friendship should be a reciprocal connection in which each person responds appropriately. Be a responsible friend.

Be a loyal friend who helps in times of need. Because you are loyal, you must also be prudent. You will be one who helps others all your life. Pray for insight and wisdom to help the right people at the right time.

Build solid relationships with those whom you can trust. You need people who honestly want the best for you.

Pray for your friends and support them with love. At times, you will find that they often aid you more readily than family members. Pray for their success and safety.

Abandon unhealthy friendships. You cannot expect to improve your life while staying connected to those whose weaknesses exceed yours.

Play an active role in the welfare of your friends. You can experience the best in association by actively contributing to relational success. Practice the art of categorizing so that you bring out the best in others. You may set them up for failure if you expect responses outside of their capabilities.

1. Do not confide in a friend who gossips.
2. Do not loan money to a friend who has a reputation for non-payment.
3. Do not expect empathy from someone who is harsh and unfeeling.
4. Do not expect a helping hand from a friend who is unreliable.
5. Do not expect etiquette from a friend who is unrefined.

6. Do not overly trust a friend in business when there is no track record of business success.
7. Do not trust a friend with your money when they cannot be trusted with their own.
8. Do not help a friend "out" when he has no intentions of "staying out."
9. Do not leave your expensive or delicate possessions in the hands of someone who has no respect for rare things.
10. Do not project qualities that do not exist in friends.

Do not set unreasonable expectations for others. You are partly responsible should they fail you.

1. It is not the betrayer's fault for betraying you.
2. It is not a liar's fault for lying to you.
3. It is not a cheater's fault for cheating you.
4. It is not a thief's fault for stealing from you.
5. It behooves you to continue this list.

Con artists need your trust. All they have is words so it is very important that they talk seventy percent more than you do. Examine these encounters carefully.

Recognize jealousy in its many forms. Every gift you have or talent you display will invoke jealousy from those around you. These will be family, friends, colleagues and acquaintances. Pay careful attention to those who are jealous and try to avoid them when you are accomplishing great things.

People demonstrate their jealousy in three basic ways.

1. They act out, to prevent you from excelling.
2. They talk about you behind your back or attempt to discourage you with their words.
3. They refuse to support your endeavors.

Many of the people who are jealous of you do not have the skill set or talent to do what you do. If you are a great painter, you may find that most people who are jealous do not paint at all.

Stay away from those who are jealous and do not dwell on them. They are unimportant.

Please get comfortable being alone. Be the kind of person who enjoys solitude as much as companionship. You must learn to appreciate the respite of quietness.

I pray that you find as much peace and contentment alone as when surrounded by others.

RELATIONSHIPS

Stay away from people who hurt your repeatedly but say they love you. Loving does not mean that you must constantly suffer at their hands.

It is best to realize your complete wellness before you get into a serious relationship. You should read material that helps you conquer personal challenges.

Every person in your life is not essential to you. Learn to be okay without their presence. Your decision is not out of animosity or malicious intent.

You may have several best friends in your life but rarely at the same time. Good friends are rare. Best friends are next to unicorns.

You will meet unscrupulous people that you really like. Do not subscribe to the thinking that by lending your presence among them, you are doing some good in their lives.

Your giving is not a blessing to those who are takers. You are infusing yourself with a false sense of purpose for which you will not be credited but faulted for mismanagement of your resources.

The self-seeking makes attempts to gain close proximity to lay eyes upon your possessions. They desire friendship because of your beneficial resources.

Judas betrayed Jesus only once. Just because you live a life of forgiveness does not mean you must stay near malicious people who continually offend you. See betrayal as an exit sign above the door and escape impending doom.

Do not ride with thugs. Guilt by association is real and can cost you in more ways than having need of a ride. You are legally involved in whatever they do, while you are with them.

If you are in the company of someone who commits a heinous crime, get the best lawyer possible and have her go to the police with you. Clear yourself if you can. Please understand, the law views you as guilty by your presence at the scene of the crime.

When criminals get caught, they will put the blame on you, in order to go free. Son, you are not a criminal. When you put yourself in their company, you are the perfect scapegoat.

I pray that you will never experience a legal crisis because of poor decision making. I have extremely high expectations for you and your family and hope that you will set even higher standards for yourself.

CODEPENDENT RELATIONSHIPS

Examine your motives for helping. Sometimes we feel the need to help others because we want them to like us or hold us in high regard. This might reveal that you have a self-esteem issue.

Son, because you have a kind and loving heart you must learn to manage your compulsion. As you mature, you will be less compelled to rescue in an unhealthy manner. You will learn better ways to love.

When you love poorly, it always diminishes you. You harm yourself emotionally and deplete other resources.

You can suffer injury while attempting to be a knight in shining armor. Avoid helping when it hurts you.

Stay away from "takers." When you avoid them, you are not losing anything. You are gaining all the things you would have lost from needy people borrowing, begging and pilfering.

Takers feel entitled. They act as though you owe them something. Be careful about accepting gifts from them because they are "priming the pump for reciprocity." They give a little to receive a great deal in return. Put yourself under no obligation to do anything for them.

Most people are in their predicament because they refuse to change their ways. You must let them go through it. This is how they come out on the other side.

Do not rescue others from the "Hand of God." There is a higher calling when people hit rock bottom. Life is trying to get their attention and cause them to yield to a divine power and purpose. Do not make yourself an available alternative to someone making critical changes in life.

You are preventing them from maturing to the point where they have no reason to rely upon you, because times of imminent distress would not exist.

The window of change is very small. Critical times present a small opportunity for us to change our thinking and ultimately our behavior. When someone shares their hardship, be sure to encourage them and let them know how excited you are for what they will become because of their challenge.

People are resilient. They survive well beyond our great and wonderful assistance. Speak positive words and learn the power of being appropriately silent. You can be an effective presence without attempting to save the day. In fact, you don't know "what day it is" in their life.

1. It could be the day of reckoning; the day to face up to what has been avoided.
2. It could be their day of destruction; when bad living reaps what it has sewn.
3. It could be the day of deliverance; when a troubled soul surrenders.
4. It could be the day of repentance; when one apologizes for all wrongdoing.
5. It could be the day to end all days.

You just don't know.

People do not tell you the whole story. People are often in trouble because of denial so they find it next to impossible to convey the whole truth when seeking help from you. You must ask a series of questions, followed by questions about the answers they give. That will put you nearer to the real story. Decide how you can assist and what degree of assistance you will provide. Rest in the fact that there are others besides you in the network. Others will also come with aid.

DATING

Be a gentleman. Dating is meant to be a series of brief encounters to enjoy company and evaluate chemistry and character. Fight the compulsion to get physical because it defeats the purpose of the information gathering that brief encounters offer.

Dating is a great way to sharpen your listening skills. Since you are eager and attentive, pay attention to the energy you have and try your best to preserve it. Be intentional in asking context questions based upon what you hear to further the conversation. You will do well to keep this practice for the rest of your life.

Avoid the compulsion to divert every topic into a personal experience conversation. Consider yourself gifted when you achieve the ability to stay in her conversation without turning it into a monologue about some experience you had, or some pain you suffered.

Read books about dating. When dating seriously, you must be intentional about what you want to learn or discuss in your time together. There are great topics to discuss and places to go that will inspire valuable conversation.

Pay careful attention to values. Values do not lie. The two of you are not compatible when your values do not match. It does not matter that you bought cute little matching T-shirts. Discontinue the relationship or face long-term misery.

If you date seriously, stay in it long enough to experience the good and the bad. This is how you know whether you are compatible enough to survive hardships and emerge stronger and closer because of them.

Pray about the person you date. I pray that God will guide you to make decisions even when you are wholly unaware of his involvement. The person you choose is critical to the outcome of your family. It is not just your future but your children's future at stake. Your choice is critical and you need divine help.

Consider the background. Family dynamics and history are important. A dysfunctional past usually means a dysfunctional future. If your date displays no evidence for change or turning herself in a new direction, you have a poor chance of overcoming this condition.

Make it a point to avoid inappropriate touching when you date. If you touch first, your emotions go before your logic. Give yourself an opportunity to evaluate the true quality of the person apart from her physical attributes.

Don't just date. Evaluate! Refrain from intimate touching. In twelve weeks, you will have encountered enough significant information that makes you extremely thankful that you did not seek intimacy with this person. If you make it past three months, your relationship overview will tell you what topics need focused attention.

Have fun. Do things that you both enjoy. This lends to understanding compatibility.

Assess the whole picture. Do not forget what is at stake. Consider how you want your family reunions to look. Will they be classy or unbearable?

Know your strengths and weaknesses. You have faults that will not accommodate certain kinds of people in your life. Recognize your flaws without beating yourself up about it. Use your recognition to make the best decision about your prospective mate. You want to avoid inflicting undue pain on someone who attempts to love you. Sometimes people choose the wrong relationship out of obsession.

Know your likes and dislikes. Do not accept a person into your life because she is willing to go overboard in her desire for you. Make sure your desire is congruent with hers. Be honest with yourself.

Promote your strengths and work on your weaknesses.
Your dominant characteristics are most attractive and that is what brought you to this point. Relationships point out your weaknesses in a way that you would not otherwise realize. Be open to learn of them without lament. Just be conscientious about improving yourself.

Do not compromise your likes and dislikes. You will ultimately be profoundly dissatisfied when you settle for less than you really desire. This will entice you to be unappreciative and perhaps even unfaithful. You cannot logically come up with any rationale to excuse your behavior.

I pray that your dating experience teaches you more than I can articulate and that it leads to a successful future.

IT'S ABOUT LOVE

It is not logically possible to make love. You must be loved and be loving. Sex is more an act of trust than an act of love. Your partner is giving away her identity in the faith that you love her. You also trust her with your identity.

Since you can give your heart to anyone, give it to someone who has given her heart to you.

Intimacy begins with knowing a person intellectually. You rarely arrive at intellectual knowledge when you start with physical pursuits. You may have gone too far physically, before you realize the intelligence does not extend far enough.

Son, you have a great capacity to love. Make sure you love and marry someone who has a healthy capacity to love you as deeply as you love her.

Love yourself the way you want others to love you. Set the example for how you want to be loved and others must follow in your footsteps. When you love yourself, you will not settle for maltreatment or abuse. Release yourself in the most loving way possible if you are not being treated well.

Seek counseling to deepen your capacity to love and care for yourself and others. Counseling is great for self-improvement as well as crisis.

Seek to understand God's love. Make it a lifelong pursuit.

Listen. Listen. Listen. To love someone well, you must listen well. Take mental notes when they speak and respond with actions that demonstrate your attentiveness. You will be well rewarded for your attention to detail.

Learn the true meaning of love. Display the appropriate quality and the right time. You must also gain confidence in the use of tough love.

Love smartly. While one form of love is deep and limitless, another may be skeptical and filled with limitations.

Anger is a form of love. There are important times when anger is love's appropriate response.

You will find love within the realm of commitment. It is a rare quality when someone supports you in the worst times of your life. That commitment is to be rewarded during the best days of your lives.

My prayers are with you in the utmost. I desire that you be fulfilled in your pursuit of someone who will profoundly love you.

MARRIAGE

Your present health impacts the future welfare of your family. One of the biggest oversights that young men make is the consideration of future family. The way you presently live can be detrimental to the welfare of your family and this is not to be taken lightly. Drug and alcohol use are a pastime that can harm your body and your children could suffer the effects of your choices.

Birth defects and learning disabilities may be among the many results of your indiscretions and an immense amount of guilt will come with that recognition. You will have to be honest.

The most difficult conversation you will ever have is the one where you admit past imprudence to your wife. It will take a real man to concede that his inability to produce children may be due to the damage he caused to his reproductive system.

I pray that you make the best choices and never have to face this situation.

When you choose a wife, make a whole-life commitment. You must stay in relationship even when you do not feel loved or loving. Your commitment must go beyond your feelings. I cannot emphasize the importance of choosing well. She must be someone who makes a whole-life commitment to you. This is a rare treasure.

A woman who loves God will have overflowing love for you.

When you both honor God, you will have a standard to rely upon in difficult times. Challenging discussions will not grow confrontational or turn violent.

Read books that inspire you to pursue a great marriage. There will always be something to improve upon.

Marry the friend you love. It is easy to cultivate new levels of intimacy when you enjoy an incredible friendship.

Your wife will develop an unfailing trust when you demonstrate consistent reliability. Be a reliable man that removes all doubt.

Never attack your wife for her weaknesses. Your goal is to encourage her strengths and cover her deficiencies as she works to cover yours.

If your wife is honest, she will acknowledge her faults. It is very difficult to get past challenges when a spouse refuses to embrace the fact that there is a recurring issue.

If your wife is the kind of person who refuses to make necessary changes, you should have known this in the dating phase. You are expecting changes in her core values. This is almost the same as requesting a genetic mutation of her personality.

You and your wife must work together in order to realize accomplishments, great and small.

Your attentiveness is a major requirement. This is one thing that men often fail to realize. Your relationship does not maintain itself simply because you said you love her. If you are not ready to modify your life to make her your number one priority, then you are not fundamentally ready.

Ask the right questions before marrying.

1. Does she pay her bills on time?
2. Is she swamped with debt and is in need of a bail-out?

3. Does she come from a difficult family dynamic that desperately seeks rescue?
4. Where does she draw the line on ethics and values?
5. Is situational theft okay? *Can I steal it if I really need it?*
6. How does she resolve conflict?
7. Does she have respect for you and others?
8. Can she appropriately disconnect from her extended family to focus on her own?
9. Is her commitment as deep as yours?

An intelligent wife will enhance your family in ways you cannot imagine. Marry intelligence.

Try to start a family together! When you build together, your love emanates from the same place. It is easier to come to an agreement and maintain solidarity on parenting decisions.

Show exceptional love when starting with a blended family. You must love your step-children in a way that builds trust and respect. A strong communication and alliance with their mother is essential to having peace in your home.

The difference between being a great lover and a damn fool is the other person. No matter how much you give, your lover's response makes the difference. Pay attention that your love is well received and reciprocated.

Protect her with your life. This is an unspoken objective that must be preserved within your heart.

Be affectionate.

Give gifts on regular days. Be generous on random days as well as special days.

Remain committed to your relationship throughout the difficult periods when you do not feel love and joy. After you have gotten past the challenge, you will both realize that your commitment to "relationship" is powerful enough to keep you together.

Pray for your wife. Make your petitions known to her and to God.

1. Pray that your understanding be increased.
2. Pray for your awareness and growth.
3. Pray for your closeness.
4. Pray for her success.
5. Pray for her health and emotional well-being.
6. Pray for her occupational fulfillment.
7. Pray for her patience (with you).

An unfaithful spouse will drive you crazy. Your sleeping and eating patterns are disrupted. Your waking thoughts are filled with doubt and suspicion. You will suffer from a lack of productivity. Resolve your problem. Do not endure prolonged suffering.

I pray that you have a successful marriage that defies statistics to stand the test of time.

FATHERHOOD

Being a father is one of the most important roles you will ever play in your life. Come to fatherhood intentionally. Do not approach this title by accident.

Your role as a father is to provide your children with the tools they need to have productive lives. Keep in mind that they will grow to have children of their own. What you do today will impact your grandchildren tomorrow.

Teach your son how to tie a neck tie and a bow tie. These are simple tasks, but more difficult to manage without a father's input. It will be a memorable event for both of you.

Teach the appropriate styles of dress for every occasion. Your son should know how to dress for formal, business and business casual events. It is important to show him how to communicate the right message with wardrobe. Make sure he knows that you are broadening his selection rather than dictating his clothing style.

Be willing to sacrifice everything for the health and welfare of your children. You may find it necessary to give up grand opportunities to accommodate their success. Your short-term loss is their long-term gain.

Pray for your children now. Even though you may be far from having kids, pray about every aspect of their lives.

Praise your children. You are the most important person in their lives and your words are the most powerful. Praise them continually and the benefits will be shown through their accomplishments.

Be whatever it is you want your sons to become. Do not just say it, demonstrate it. Live by a set of principles that they can describe whether you speak of them or not.

As a father, you can cause more damage and destruction to children than any other person, place, or thing. The damage you cause will last for more generations than you will ever know. Have every intention of doing right by them.

Be very generous. Lavish your children with gifts and teach the responsibility of having them. In this way, they understand your love and your expectations.

Generate income for their future. Do not be so caught up in their day-to-day survival that you fail them tomorrow. Have a college savings plan.

One day, your son will start a family and then his son will start a family. Your legacy begins today and their destiny is dependent upon you. Your family will be a reflection of the wonderful things you did or all that you failed to do.

Please make it your goal to do right by your family. They deserve your love and sacred devotion.

Design a family crest. Include emblems that exemplify the values you want your descendants to maintain. Have an insignia for your faith, a symbol for education, business and other ideals. Create a logo for marriage and family values.

Host an annual dinner where you celebrate your family's history or the making of a better one. If there is no triumph, then tell of the family failures that you are determined not to repeat.

Start new traditions for your family. Have a private ceremony for sons crossing over into manhood. Include prominent men who possess the character that you want your sons to emulate. They will be reminded of the cloud of witnesses watching their progress.

Create a ceremony for your daughter where you convey the importance of giving her heart to the right man.
Remind her that with valor, you demonstrated the qualities that she is to look for in a man and if he lacks any of these, he should also lack her presence in his life.

Be a sentinel for your children. Stand guard over them and respond to every threat to their physical, emotional and psychological wellbeing. Offer them the ultimate security of knowing how much you love them.

Pronounce a blessing. Rest your hand on the crown of their heads and ask for continued blessings.

1. Thank God for the special characteristics of each child.
2. Pray for their safety.
3. Pray for their success.
4. Thank God for giving them to you.

We act out of that which we know. Whatever I did in my limited knowledge was riddled with mistakes. You can learn from these.

I pray that you maintain the energy it takes to be a great father.

WORK

Work hard at every endeavor you have chosen to engage. No matter how difficult the task, you can walk away knowing that you did well.

When a job is unfulfilling, be thankful for a paycheck. Under certain conditions, there is nothing more to be had. In this case, give only that which is required and find another place to contribute your time, talent and resources.

First, do what must be done. When you procrastinate, the pain lasts longer than it would while you were completing the task.

Constantly educate yourself so that you can take full advantage of unique employment opportunities. If you play music but you studied marketing, you might end up in the promotions department of a giant record company. You will be surprised by the number of high paying, fun jobs that come before you. Be surprised but also be prepared.

A Master's degree will open many more doors for you. You enable yourself to grasp more opportunities, having shown that you are capable of learning and executing at a higher level. It is possible that you may work in an entirely different occupation than your degree field.

Learn to negotiate completely devoid of emotions. Use your intelligence to accomplish principled negotiations in which everyone achieves a reasonable portion of their desires. These situations require strategic thinking. Emotions will derail your ability to process logically.

Use your creativity and intelligence to make mediocre products great. Rely upon your logic and you will tend to be less emotionally tied to your work. In this way, you will enable yourself to make improvements on even products that you deem to be adequate for the market. This is how you reinvent yourself and your products.

Success comes because of many failures. Failure is acceptable because it is an attempt to succeed. For this reason, I hope you experience a series of failures.

Keep a record of your failures and learn to appreciate them for the lessons they teach. The person with the most failures is often the one with the most success.

Do not be afraid to make business decisions. You must make decisions based upon the information you have at the time. This is called a business premise. Pay attention to the results of your premises so you can make the proper adjustments for future success.

Build a network of colleagues who are successful. When you need to find work, you will have excellent leads and opportunities. You will also have excellent service when you need something done.

Return phone calls the same day you receive them. Do not let this busy day overlap another busy day.

Be on time. Be early so that you can relax and breathe easy. Keep your heart rate and your stress levels low. Make timeliness a part of your excellent reputation.

Find a quiet place to meditate on what you want to accomplish for the day. Think about the tools you will need and the time you must invest for completion. Pray for your daily success. Think about it, and then execute it. This is a form of prayer and meditation.

Consider the risk. Every business endeavor has known and unknown risks that cost money. Do your best to anticipate problems and generate solutions.

Always communicate effectively with those with whom you need to work to achieve success. Try to communicate early and often. Then confirm what has been communicated.

Write great business communications. When you write well, the reader can focus on the important ideas you want to convey.

Send "Thank You" cards. People appreciate the effort you make.

Consistently reward your employees. People are inspired to do great work for your company when they know you appreciate their high level of proficiency.

Finance

Money management reveals your readiness for life. Poor management announces that you will suffer and suffer often. I pray for your success and hope you realize the need for great stability with your family.

The world operates on Finance, Insurance and Real Estate. These are the industries where major resources are generated. Produce wealth by working in one of these fields or a tributary of their revenue streams.

Learn the rule of seventy-two.

Practice the art of budgeting. It may be a chore at first but it will pay dividends in a short time. Pay careful attention to where your money goes and you will have the power to decide what is most and least important. You can always adjust your plan.

Keep a significant portion of your income within your possession. Shift your attitude so that you see spending as a losing proposition. In this case, it is not how much you win but how little you lose.

A low savings account balance is an indication that you do not think highly of yourself. Your checking account reflects the things you value. Your savings account reflects how much you value yourself.

Save your money for big items and events. Stop spending on small things that are meaningless. You may wake up one day to realize that your life only amounts to the small trinkets you have collected.

Create a savings plan! Every time you get paid, move the previous balance from checking to savings. Then move your savings to a money market account. Get stocks and mutual funds.

Pay your bills on time. Pay your bills ahead of time and amortize your debt as often as possible.

Avoid credit card debt. Until the mid-nineteenth century, debtor's prison existed for those who could not pay their bills. People were incarcerated in workhouses until their debt was paid. Credit card debt is its own prison. Just like jail-time, excessive debt is an entrapment that may incarcerate you for extended periods of your life.

Use secured loans to build wealth. You would rarely default on a loan to yourself. This is a great way to increase discipline and avoid credit card debt. Put up your money and borrow the bank's money against it. When the loan is paid off, you will get your money back, less the low interest you paid on the loan. Your credit score goes up.

Own a home. Start humbly with a place that is easy to pay for so you can amortize the debt. By paying off your debt early, you can move on to bigger and better property while renting the home you own.

Do not spend all your resources on one property, attempting to impress your neighbors and strangers who pass by. Purchase several properties that produce income.

Build a summer home, tiny house or cabin. Have a getaway place within a few hours driving distance so you can create a vacation atmosphere any time you desire.

Be prudent when aiding with money. It is honorable to lend financial support but make sure it does not turn into financial maintenance. You have your own set of budgetary concerns. The actions of your youth are directly related to the quality of success in your later years. You must believe that your financial habits have an impact upon your family even though you may be single. Live as though you have greater responsibilities beyond yourself.

Never co-sign for a loan!

Never co-sign for a loan. This is a rule you must follow. The person who asks this of you is not stable enough to close a financial deal on their own. There is a reason for this. It is not so much the present circumstances but the life-style choices that have existed for a very long time. Do not attempt to fix it. People are resilient. They always find a way to succeed in the face of their challenges.

When you cosign for a loan, the debt belongs to you. Never cosign for a loan.

Maintain a budget. Keep up with your spending so that you know which categories are failing. Make necessary adjustments and accommodations; tighten up here and loosen up there.

Treat money management as an occupation and a primary purpose in your life. You will most often have what you need when you manage what you have.

Money management tells you whether you are in the right occupation. Sometimes, the jobs we love do not compensate well enough to sustain us. Critical choices must be made to achieve financial and life goals. Be courageous to make changes.

Get a financial advisor you trust and maintain a lifelong relationship.

Make sure that your wants never outweigh your needs.

Hire an accountant. They understand your financial picture and can assist with present and future endeavors.

Budget for life insurance. This is an essential asset for your family.

The compulsion to impress other people is an extremely expensive disorder. If you are spending money just to receive a compliment from people, something is wrong with your thinking. Seek professional counseling. I say that seriously. Get some help.

Partition your income. Try to use only fifty-percent of your earnings. This will shift your spending, saving and investment habits. You will increase your net worth when you control spending.

Learn to negotiate a higher pay rate by perceiving a lower dollar-value. When you consider the dollar's value as sixty-percent, you are compelled to negotiate for a forty-percent increase.

Raise your bottom line, monthly. Increase the amount you are left with after expenses are paid. This will raise your net worth.

Advance yourself slowly and methodically. Patience is required, no matter what your income level.

Reward yourself for doing well financially. You can afford things that are well built and long-lasting.

Pay attention to human nature as well as financial trends when you invest. All data should inform your strategies.

Pray for the advancement of your skills, then do your part. You are infused with the courage to move forward. It is up to you to achieve financial success.

RESPONSIBILITY

Responsibility is like a title-deed. It is yours because your name is on it.

1. It is yours in which to care.
2. It is yours to maintain.
3. Whatever it costs, you pay the price.
4. Whatever its dividends, you benefit primarily.

Do not blame others for failures over which you had control. One of the measurements of your manhood is tied to your ability to take ownership of undesirable outcomes.

Divorce yourself from feelings when having to perform a difficult task. Your feelings will deter you from doing what needs to be done. You will have more failures than successes simply because you did not feel like succeeding.

When you delegate, the responsibility still rests with you. All outcomes are attributed to you. Stay connected to those to whom you delegate tasks. Support and guide as necessary.

Be a finisher.

1. Use a project management system.
2. Divide your work into phases.
3. Treat every task as a project.
4. Employ the right people.
5. Put tasks in order.
6. Pick an approach for each task; hands-on or delegate.
7. Work with deadlines.
8. Evaluate progress.
9. Have built-in time for correction and quality assurance.
10. Manage risks.
11. Rest: Give yourself time to review the finished product.
12. Reveal: Present your product to the world.

You can be confident of the quality and totality of your work when you use a systematic process.

Multi-tasking requires various levels of thinking and problem solving skills. Practice multitasking so you can learn to make assessments and revisions in real-time. Companies will pay you handsomely for this ability.

Finish well. Bring your projects to completion. After a small number of project finishes, you will come to love the journey, perhaps more than the release party.

Consider using my Ai-T.O.D. (A-Todd) System for daily preparation. (Auto-imperative Things of the Day)

Auto-imperatives are the things you hold as important, regardless of any other tasks or projects. Your list may look like this:

1. Devote time to prayer and meditation.
2. Eat a healthy breakfast.
3. Exercise at home or the gym.
4. Review your schedule for the day.
5. Communicate daily goals to family.
6. Be liquid so that you can pour yourself into urgent matters that arise without warning.
7. Gradually add to your list of auto-imperatives.

I pray for your ability to respond appropriately to all the responsibilities in your life.

BUSINESS

Be honest in your business dealings. It is not necessary to cheat people to advance yourself.

Never sway from honest dealings even when pressed by difficult circumstances. Your character is directly related to your business practices. Choose to operate with integrity rather than compromise.

Become a great communicator by increasing your vocabulary. This enables you to draw images with words. When your vocabulary is limited, the listener must work to fill in the blanks.

Talk socially before you negotiate. Discover hometowns, common hobbies and favorite vacation spots. The smallest commonalities will help you close big deals.

When you are having difficulty asking your price, pause or end the conversation. Give yourself time to process. Sometimes, the silence will cause the buyer to offer more than you would have asked, had you spoken.

Your asking price is practical, not emotional. Do not attempt to be well liked for charging low prices. There is a class of people who appreciate fine service and are willing to pay for it.

Learn the art of negotiation. They call it an art form for a reason.

Be courageous to start a business rooted in innovation. Consumers will buy your products because they aspire to be enhanced by them.

Pursue a degree in business.

Be eager to take on new opportunities. As an intelligent man, you can cross-train in new roles that expand your understanding and your income.

Everything that glitters probably has glitter on it. Beware of opportunities that exceed reality. Calm your excitement and ask tough questions. Research may show that the offer is inflated or fraudulent.

Pay attention to misleading language or too many words uttered. Those are the elements of deception.

Be careful of those whose laughter is inauthentic, when negotiating. Although the person could simply be nervous, this could be a signal for deception.

Be careful not to celebrate your deals before they have proven legitimate.

Be reliable and your business will thrive. Providing dependable service is a dying art. Capitalize in areas where other businesses fail.

Join elite business organizations so that you can learn from the best. Your presence informs others that you have a desire to succeed.

TRAVEL

Take your family on vacations regularly. It is important that you build fond memories.

Get away at least once every year. You need to recharge your battery.

1. Travel to beaches where you can look out upon the horizon and wonder how sailors had the courage to take to the sea.
2. Spend time in the mountains so that you can breathe fresh air at high altitudes and experience the wonderment of creation.
3. Visit wide-open vistas where you grant your eyes an opportunity to see a rain storm, as it travels, from twenty miles away.

Travel expands your understanding of the world.

Travel rejuvenates your mind. Grant yourself freedom from daily responsibilities.

Travel to meet new people and reconnect with family and friends who live abroad.

Travel to gain an understanding of cultures and acclimate yourself to new places.

Become an experienced traveler. An informed traveler is unafraid to connect with local inhabitants who enhance the quality of your visit.

Visit exotic places. A great deal of preparation and planning has taken place when you visit Tahiti or Tonga. Give yourself beautiful vacations like these.

Always study locations before you visit. Read maps and browse web sites to gather information. Acclimate yourself to a new city by knowing the transit system. This information will increase your comfort level.

Pack thoroughly and leave for the airport as early as possible. You want to relax and let go, from the moment you leave home.

Play local gigs all over the country. Stay in contact with your college friends and play gigs when you visit their various cities. Over the next twenty years, you will become a national entity from having introduced yourself locally, all over the nation.

I pray that you will take time to see the world and expand your connection to it.

NUTRITION

Drink water as your preferred beverage.

Drink distilled water. Hospital grade water is distilled water. This is the water for life. You must look out for yourself because manufacturers only care that you buy their products. It does not matter whether it is or is not best for you.

Cleanse yourself regularly. Consider different kinds of programs from liquid diets to fasting. Give your body the same opportunity to thrive as you are giving your career.

Eat healthy foods to avoid ingesting toxins. Detoxing your body requires courage and commitment. Put this on your calendar and execute it with boldness.

Abstain from fast foods. Fast food is big business but not necessarily big on nutrition. If you are always eating on the run, then perhaps you are running too much.

When you buy groceries, purchase more foods from the outer walls than you acquire down the aisles. The freshest groceries and organic foods are mostly along the walls, while the dry goods and preserved items are in the aisles.

Practice good eating habits so that your children will do the same. Read cookbooks and nutritional guides for assistance.

Use honey, apple cider vinegar, turmeric, ginger and other organic foods for their benefits. You will acquire a very fulfilling diet.

Enjoy fruits and vegetables from around the world. There are so many wonderful foods to which you have never been exposed. Gain new experiences.

Eat at high-end restaurants for better quality foods. The value to your body is worth the cost to your wallet.

Purchase organic groceries. Feed yourself better and you will perform at your best.

Protect yourself. It is your responsibility.

Shop for the better item, not the lowest cost. You deserve the best in everything you do, including the foods you eat.

Get to know a nutritionist. This is someone who gives personalized assistance for your specific circumstances. You deserve it.

Avoid processed sugar. The body has no need of it. Guard your children's consumption of processed sugar. You are working to protect their childhood and adulthood.

Snack on fruits, veggies and snack bars. Eat walnuts, cashews, peanuts, sunflower seeds and things of this nature. You are satisfying your hunger while endowing your body with power to meet its requirements.

Do not use recreational drugs. The moment you give in to this practice is the moment you lose control of your liberty. Drugs dictate your priorities and schedule. You will find that there is more recreation than vocation taking place in your life. It would be sad to think yourself liberated while suffering the loss of liberty from drug use.

Do not rationalize questionable habits. You are responsible for your health and welfare, so do not attempt to justify a faulty rationale.

Remember that you are chosen by God.

The rules and repercussions that do not apply to others most certainly apply to you. You can never get away with doing the things that others do wrong. (Stop complaining about it. You are chosen).

Love yourself. Be very kind to your body.

I pray that you master the art of nutrition.

FITNESS AND HEALTH

Exercise routinely. Have a regimen that covers the entire body. Get a membership or join a group devoted to a certain kind of training. You are offering your machine the best operating conditions.

Fitness is a great way to enjoy the outdoors.

1. You will be inspired to travel if you take up kayaking.
2. You will learn survival skills when you go camping.
3. You will see your city from a different perspective when you ride bike trails.
4. You will strengthen your inner-core while water skiing.
5. You can maximize your coordination when snow skiing.
6. Strengthen your lung capacity and breathing by hiking mountain trails.

Train in a boxing gym. In a very short time, you will realize what it takes to be in fighting condition. This is also a great way to build a physical toughness that can be applied to other aspects of your life.

Embrace a physical activity that you really enjoy. This is a great way to commit to exercise.

Be intentional about gaining friendships with exercise enthusiasts. Friends inspire you to continue when you would otherwise be bored or tired. You also have the bonus of being with experienced people.

Build alliances with those who push you to get better. Encouragement and exercise go together.

Exercise when you are under pressure or suffering from stress. This is a great way to push back against the challenges that are pushing against you.

Have regular physicals and checkups with your doctor. Once you are on the right fitness path, your doctor visits will only be for small shifts in direction.

Keep regular dental appointments and maintain your dental health between visits. You are maintaining a standard for yourself and setting one for your children.

Every man will face challenges that weigh heavily on his mind. When you are suffering, seek the counsel of good men who recognize your pain. They can talk you through it and help you emerge better on the other side of your difficulty.

If emotional agony persists, seek professional help. Since men are compelled to solve their own problems, you may grow compulsive enough to act out against yourself and others.

Set up a magnificent wall of defense when fighting depression. Eat healthy meals, exercise vigorously and guard your time for sleep. Set goals that give meaning and purpose to your life.

Take vitamins and supplements that are known to aid in treating depression.

Talk with your doctor. There are medications that help to fight depression. Consider the benefits and the known side-effects when making a decision.

Do not allow suicide to become an option. This is a terrible attempt at solving a temporary problem with a permanent solution. When you are suicidal, you feel hopeless. If I could stop the world from turning, I would freeze time and ask you to write the names of the many people of which your life brings hope. You will quickly realize that suicide is selfish. Your life is valuable to others, even though you may not presently find value for yourself.

You have no idea of the many lives you can save by telling the personal story of the time that you were not willing to preserve your own life. Since we all survive on hope, your experience is invaluable to the hopeless.

I pray that you always find the courage to embrace life with all its changes, challenges and victories.

Religion

Treat your belief as a philosophy, not a religion. Philosophy is for the thinking man. When you understand Scripture, you will have guiding principles. With religion, you form habits that may or may not be based upon anything factual.

Act upon your philosophy. As your thinking improves, so should your actions.

The only way to know the Most-High God is to read the Bible. Study to get the underlying meaning. That is where the truth resides. A great deal of what you hear may be conjecture and assumption. You can do better than this.

Take a Hermeneutics class. This class will teach you the correct way to interpret Scripture.

Learn to exegete a biblical text. Study Greek and Hebrew even if you only reach novice level. Your understanding will be above average.

Be a great representative. People respect you for maintaining your philosophy even when they do not share your beliefs.

When you pursue God, you will often find that you are walking alone. The people you encounter at the far end of the path are infinitely better than those you left behind. Just keep walking.

Seek answers from God. Everyone has thoughts and opinions that are metaphysical but God's logic answers every metaphysical question. You will have a profound understanding of life's questions when you gain a deeper relationship with God.

Do not wait for a speaker on a platform to decipher logos for you. It may be a while before he approaches the topic for which you need answers.

Please do not attend churches that are disorganized, unfriendly or old fashioned. God is found on the cultural edge. Churches that refuse to change are also those that refuse to grow. You will not thrive in places like these.

Do not follow leaders who have less intelligence than you. Their lack of refinement will be the excuse to keep you from excelling in the confines of their ministry. It is human nature for leaders to want everyone to follow them no matter how far behind they have fallen.

Do not reduce your intelligence to accommodate someone else's lack. When you attend an intelligent church, you are free to use your intellect without facing jealousy and constraint.

Beware of churches that over-emphasize the supernatural, miraculous attributes of God above all else. These are the kinds of places that are more consumed with what God is saying (prophetically) than what he has already said scripturally. I agree that God is prophetic, supernatural, miraculous and more.

God originally revealed himself to those who were often uneducated and perhaps illiterate, so it was imperative to demonstrate his power by doing miraculous things. In the Old Testament, God's people were experiencing the word more than reading the word. They were better able to understand God when he revealed himself supernaturally.

Today, we are literate. We can read and the benefit of the written document. We are literate, but lazy. Our laziness creates underachievement in biblical education and understanding.

You will experience God supernaturally by reading his word and living a principled life of integrity.

Attend a church that celebrates your gifts and abilities.

Avoid church people who are jealous and small-minded. The longer you stay around them, the more like them you become.

When you attend a great church, you feel great about your financial support.

Your honest self-assessment makes you more prone to be honest with God. This is all it really takes to get better at life.

Confess who you are, not just what you have done. God will forgive you for what you have done, but He can only deal with who you are if you get real about it. He needs your cooperation and will never attempt to transform the part of yourself that you are hiding.

It is better to be forthright with yourself and others. This is the straightest path to your ultimate destination – maturity.

Society is changing. Culture, community and people are changing for the worse. It will become more and more acceptable in the view of the culture to do the wrong thing.

Do not compromise the meaning of right and wrong. If you taint the meaning and distort the boundaries, your assessment will become skewed.

Examine your life against the ways of God, not society. God is still the measurement for righteousness, regardless of how open society becomes to doing wrong. I pray that your relationship with God is authentic and personal.

WORSHIP

Let worship take place in your heart and soul. This is where you will meet with God.

Attend a regular place of authentic worship.

Do not pretend piety. Be honest with God. Avoid any attempts to fit in with people by pretending to be more deeply devoted than you really are. You may come to realize that you are pretending in order to blend with people who are pretending as well.

God reveals himself to those who seek him. Go after God by reading the word and practicing godly principles.

Retain friends who hold sacred the value of righteous living.

Observe a daily time of prayer. Maintain a sacred space.

Worship always. Present yourself in a manner that brings honor. This does not require god-language or an abnormally pious presentation but humility and grace.

Be grateful. None of us are worthy of the things we have yet we are blessed.

Worship with a deep sense of appreciation for all that God has done in your life.

Be sincere. God understands your skepticism and doubt. Your honesty merges with God's ability to meet you at the crossroads. When you ask for help with your unbelief, you will receive more than requested.

Trust God even when you are broken. This is when you acquire your deepest faith.

Trust God even though you may not sense his presence. There are seasons when you lose sensitivity. This is the meaning of faithfulness. You serve faithfully, not feelingly.

Honor the Lord. Authenticity is important to God so make your vertical praise coincide with your day-to-day activities.

My prayers are with you in this life-long endeavor.

PHILOSOPHY

Cultivate a deep love for wisdom. This is the meaning of philosophy.

Get to know the great philosophers and their premises. You can follow the advancement of logical thought by learning the basics about Thales, Socrates, Plato, Aristotle and others. The more informed you become, the less room you will leave for illogical thinking.

Love wisdom in its many forms. When you encounter foreign cultures, embrace practices that are profitable to you. Consider their diets and exercise habits.

Be a kind and patient listener when others share their ideas, no matter how different they are from your own. You will increase your understanding of worldviews and those who embrace them. Listen for logic and contradiction without interruption.

Mark flawed logic but do not engage in argument. Build a relationship where opportunity exists to subtly compare your ideas.

People who are seeking an understanding should find it when they encounter you. Use your knowledge to advance others.

Philosophy – everybody has one. People have a collection of opinions that form a philosophy. Much of it can be driven by misguided ideology. This is how we justify bigotry, bias and just about any position we hold dear.

Be a man of justice. Be fair when the power is in your hands.

CREATIVITY

Creativity is godly. Every time you create, you are emulating your Creator.

Creativity begins in chaos. You must call your creative chaos into order with a systematic approach for success.

Treat every creative idea as though it is a project that brings chaos into your life. A great deal of your world is in disarray until you bring your ideas to completion.

The more ideas you launch at one time, the more chaos you invite into your life. It is better to manage one project and the list of tasks that come along with it than be overwhelmed by unfinished goals.

A cluttered room is the perfect example of multiple incomplete tasks. A cluttered vehicle is also a sign of all the different tasks and trips you made without resetting.

Write or record all your creative ideas no matter how zany or farfetched. Crazy ideas spark usable innovations that generate unbelievable results.

Publish a book of all your ideas so that others may benefit from the concepts you would never get around to launching. You will still be compensated for your intelligence, even when you do not bring your thoughts to fruition.

Be very careful about launching too many projects at one time. Remember, you are creating something out of nothing but chaos and disarray.

Build a team. Put the right people around you and make sure they are finishers with a track record. When you are the visionary, there is no need for more visionaries. You would stand around daydreaming or talking of creative ways to accomplish your goals without accomplishing anything.

1. Acquire good workers.
2. Hire great managers who maintain your vision.
3. Get people who can engineer creative ways to implement your ideas.
4. Recruit effective communicators who can keep a team on track without insulting anyone.

Do not be afraid to fail. When you fall on your face, you get up on your knees. By the time you stand again, you will have gained three feet just from falling.

Failure informs success. Failing teaches valuable lessons. Remember them well.

LEADERSHIP

Pursue leadership positions as soon as possible. Do not underestimate your ability to lead simply because you are younger or new to an organization. Your communications and problem-solving skills qualify you for the higher pursuit.

A leader must stay ahead. You must learn leadership principles and continually hone your skills to maintain your relevance as a leader.

Remove yourself from operations guided by a poor leader. You deserve smart leadership that does not waste your time and energy. If the quality of leadership is unworthy of your time and talent, just release yourself without complaint.

Be careful with your comments that discredit an organization. People who find the organization profitable may perceive you simply to be disgruntled.

Lead well. Leadership is a position of leverage that grants you the capacity to impact people's lives in a meaningful way. Use your leverage to do some good in the world.

Street gangs have leaders but the destruction they cause can never be associated with truly leading well.

Do not be a person who has low competency while aspiring to be in charge. When your ego is greater than your leadership ability, it is the beacon of your narcissism.

When you lead friends, require more from them than others. Their respect for you will assist in building trust with everyone else who follows. When a friend fails to support your leadership, he also fails as a friend.

Be thoughtful. Consider the implications of your plans and be agile enough to make rapid critical changes.

Be decisive. Commit to a decision. After weighing your options, make a single choice. Stand by your decision and learn from the results. Start by having a decisive aim.

Study leadership and attend workshops where you learn from the best in the business. Great leadership does not happen by osmosis but by intentional pursuit of information and practice. Read everything you can about leadership and you will be amazed how refined your skills become.

Lead with your intellect and not your ego. People can spot the difference. Even though your charisma generates followers, your intelligence produces retention.

Build a team of potential leaders. Great teams are important in almost everything you do. Even your wife and children must work as a team. Be intentional to reproduce great leaders.

Lead with an open hand. Do not be so stuck on your ideas that no one else's thinking is important. Your arrogance prevents others from showing their intelligence. As a rule, you must allow others to implement their ideas as frequently as possible. When you lead with an open hand, the results will be bigger and better.

Celebrate your accomplishments so that achievement becomes a way of life.

Take a leadership role, when the opportunity presents itself. It is rewarding to see the result of your efforts. Since you are valuable, you might as well be valuable to as many people as possible.

Lend your time and talents to the best opportunities.

TENACITY

Push yourself to accomplish as many of your personal goals as possible. Just think, when you are under someone else's authority, you accomplish every assigned task for them. Use that same tenacity to realize your own achievements.

Never give up on worthy endeavors. Put up a fight to reach your goals. Achievement requires struggle.

Choose goals that you can accomplish without having to rely upon others. You will finish without external errors or delays. It will be a welcome contribution when people come along-side to assist.

You are unique! The more you realize this, the better you will understand why people do not fully get you or your ideas. Move forward with little need for outside encouragement. People will always understand after you have reached your goal.

Go away quietly with the resolve to do what others say cannot be done. Why argue with anyone who does not have the capacity to facilitate innovative thoughts. What would be the point? It is better to show than to tell.

When speaking with a company representative who is unable to give you the result you need, push the elevator button. Always have a mind to go up. As a consumer, you have access to higher levels than the employee has probably ever been within the company. You can get to the top and communicate with people that they may only hope to encounter at the Christmas party. Be polite but persistent. Your money and customer loyalty matters.

Make progress. You will always see things from a new vantage point that could not be seen, had progress not taken you down the road. The end-product will be immensely better because of the decisions and adjustments you are able to make.

Take the initiative. Always find a solution or an ingenious approach to resolve an issue. Perceive challenges before anyone else does. Companies pay you a great deal of money for intuition and unique problem-solving skills. You are a consultant.

I pray that you speak with clarity and stand with courage at every opportunity.

DO IT NOW

There are things that must be done right now. Do it now.

There is a perpetual "to-do" list in your life. The things that are most important should emerge as priorities in your heart.

Make three levels of priority:

1. Level One – What's Hot (do it right now)
2. Level Two – What's Next (do it next)
3. Level Three – What's on the Radar (Do it later)

Never perform level-three priorities on a whim. There are tasks to do now and next. When you close out high-priority tasks, the lower priorities emerge as high-level tasks.

Time is always limited. Consider all the things that must be done and grant each endeavor an allotment of time. When time expires, move on so that you do not hinder your overall achievement.

When you "do it now," you afford yourself ample time for analysis and revision. When you procrastinate, there is hardly any time left to check for quality assurance.

Clean your room! This is something that we men tend to deem unimportant but this is your first place of retreat. It should be the quiet place to escape from clutter in the world. You cannot have peace and clutter in the same room.

Clean out your car! Every time you stop, remove something that does not need to be there. Wash and wax regularly. This will help you notice tire pressure, broken lenses and other critical changes in your vehicle.

Clean your home! A good way to assure a clean home is to have regular socials with guest that you respect highly. You will create a great environment and be pleased with the cleaning habits you form.

If you struggle with cleaning, take pictures of your space. Pictures reveal clutter in ways that you may not perceive and they give you an idea of what visitors see when they enter your home.

I pray that the conviction of the Lord will help you to do the right things at the right time, every time.

KNOW GOD'S GRACE

Do not hold onto things of which God has already let go.

Forgive yourself even though you may face consequences for what you have done.

Be human. They make mistakes.

Knowing God's grace is how you learn to offer grace to others.

Many of my choices turned out to be the wrong decision. You will have to make the corrections for my failures.

I was honest with you about my life. The adverse effects of my abusive father impacted you as well. Seek God's love to fill the void that was created.

Take the truth that I offered you and find effective solutions for your emotional and psychological wellness. You have the power of knowing.

You do not have to decipher the ugly truth or process the pain of some newly discovered ghost from our past. You know what to work on. Now, go work on it.

Go with God. You can conquer your challenges with God's help.

Lay it all before God. Have the courage to approach God with every challenge you face.

1. Your character
2. Your integrity
3. Your honesty and dishonesty
4. Your love and selfishness

5. Your procrastination
6. Your self-esteem
7. Your hidden sins
8. Your obvious flaws

His grace saved your life. His grace keeps you in love. His grace forgave you and continues to do so. His grace blesses you.

Knowing God's grace helps you to forgive yourself. If God forgives you, who are you to withhold forgiveness from yourself?

You will always get through it. No matter what, you will always get through it.

Sometimes, the people closest to you are those who cause the deepest pain. Here is what you should understand when you suffer this way:

1. God uses pain to help you make progress.
2. People can only stab you in the back when they are in striking distance.
3. The greatest pain can be derived from people you really trust.
4. You are always better and wiser after your challenge.

You will suffer loss. You will lose money, items of value, important documents, jobs and friends. You will even lose loved ones but you will survive and be transformed by every loss.

I expect you to excel because it is within you to do so.

Dealing with adversity is a big part of adulthood. You must overcome every challenge set before you.

I worked very hard on your behalf. This book is a small representation of my labor toward your success.

Seek reliable family and friends during difficult times.

Only share your heart with a few listeners who really care. Although your friends care about you, they still have difficulty understanding your pain at the deepest level. They will become exasperated while you remain unfulfilled with their counsel.

Do not avoid pain. Process it. You will always be stronger and smarter because of your trial.

Grace will sustain you through all your trials. Grace is one of the most powerful concepts you will ever experience.

I pray that you come into a full comprehension of God's grace and that it compels you to undertake a role that involves bringing others into the same understanding.

BEING ALONE

Learn to love flying solo.

Alone is where you find peace and quiet. You will never achieve the quality of quietness that you gain from being alone. That is the only time you can have control over your silence.

You are healthy and whole when you can enjoy being alone as much as interacting with others. Love yourself enough to spend time with "you."

Take advantage of the opportunity to complete unfinished goals.

Find a great hobby. Set aside a regular time for indulging in a cool diversion.

Shut down and rest. Close off from everything to get the rest you need.

Take time to watch shows you normally miss.

Consider being alone as being "all one." You are happy and whole.

OPINIONS

A person's opinion should matter only when derived from intelligent thought.

Opinions should matter when they are honestly intended to help you. Be grateful and gracious to acknowledge the intent. Then, use all your data to make the best possible decision.

Beware of ideas offered by those with limited knowledge on the subject. Theirs may be founded upon guesswork.

Too much interference makes it difficult to find the right answer.

There are unlimited correct answers. There may be several ideas that work well. This is when you get the luxury of choice.

Criticism is always critical. Criticism often takes an opportunity to make personal attacks while critiquing the product or result.

Critical analysis is more valuable than criticism.

1. Critical analysis searches for facts.
2. Critical analysis seeks positive answers.
3. Critical analysis isolates the main idea from anything personal.
4. Critical analysis finds weaknesses and offers solutions.
5. Critical analysis generates many ideas.
6. Critical analysis makes good products better.

EDUCATION

Educate yourself. It is the most important thing you can do in life. Sometimes we fail to realize the importance of learning until it is painfully late. I want you to get it while you have ample time.

Ignorance is more expensive than an education.

Teachers are like spotters at a gym. They offer exposure and inspiration. Give yourself at least two hours of study time for every hour spent in the classroom. This is how you distinguish yourself from other learners. You will have a superior understanding.

Pursue education so that you know what it feels like to defeat the greatest challenge in life – ignorance.

Join a study group to increase your success. This is a great way to correct mistakes. You can get a better understanding by comparing notes.

People will pay for your intelligence. When you learn things that the general population does not know, your intellect becomes a valuable commodity.

1. Learn to do graphic design.
2. Learn how to print posters and signage.
3. Work for an advertising agency.
4. Learn to record and mix audio.
5. Record podcasts for aspiring broadcasters.
6. Produce voice-overs for business owners.
7. Learn search-engine optimization.
   a. Every person with a web site will need your service.
   b. You can work for Google.
8. Learn how to restore classic cars.

    a. Every car you touch will compensate you handsomely.
    b. People will come from near and far to do business with you.

When you find your interest, get to know more about it than anyone else in your field. Your expertise is valuable in more ways than you can imagine and there is no limit to the kinds of opportunities you will have.

1. People will pay just to talk to you on the phone.
2. Companies will pay your travel expenses and fees to have you consult them for a week.
3. Viewers will pay a monthly subscription to watch your teaching videos.
4. You can have a syndicated radio show or a television show.

The capacity to understand and understanding are not the same thing. Your capacity tells me that you are highly capable of learning, but that does not guarantee the acquisition of knowledge.

1. You must attend college or receive specialized training in some field of interest.
2. You must continue to learn throughout your career.
3. You must cross-train so that you can change occupations.
4. You should study topics of interest beyond your job.
5. You must enhance yourself always.
6. You must come to realize that no matter how much you know, there is still a lot to learn.
7. You should be the person to whom others turn for knowledge and advice.
8. You must be equal to the top professionals in your field.
9. You must earn the respect of others for your authentic intelligence.

Pursue education so that you understand how to transport your children from challenge to success.

Become an educator. Do not be arrogant in your understanding but use it to enhance others.

Take advantage of studying abroad. You can expand your understanding while becoming globally competitive. It is also a great way to vacation.

I love books. I hope you develop the same appreciation for them.

Take college trips with your kids when they get to high school. Give them an opportunity to mentally frame a real picture of college campuses. It will give them a tangible goal that adds to the value your family has for education.

To increase your success rate, talk with parents who are successfully educating their children. Parents could use a real network where they share information and experiences.

Push through the worn-out period. There will be times when you are completely exhausted in pursuit of your goal and it is easy to become bored after the sixty percent mark. This is when you must redouble your effort, knowing that there are benefits to finishing your journey.

Fall in love with the finish line. Once you know what it feels like to achieve a major goal, become a collector of finished products. Get a second degree or write volume two of your novel.

I pray for your success, protection, and the discipline it takes in order to finish well.

MILITARY SERVICE

Serve as a commissioned officer. This requires a college degree and brings a dramatic change to your career path, quality of your service, and pay grade. Enlisted service men will render their salutes to you and show the utmost respect.

Serve in a military occupation that grants access to the latest technology. Civilian companies will be eager to hire you because of your training, discipline, and knowledge.

Consider the sacrifice when you serve. With all the benefits comes the responsibility of deploying for combat at a moment's notice. It may be necessary to sacrifice your life.

You will make life-long friends in the service.

Every kind of person you will meet in the world is also on the military base. There are murderers, liars and thieves serving in the military right now. Be ever watchful of those around you.

Military prisons are in full operation. When you are charged with a military crime, you are guilty until you prove yourself innocent. This is a difficult truth.

Serve well, follow orders and always be on time.

Take advantage of all the benefits that military service offers. Do not wait until you are a veteran. There are wonderful opportunities available while on active duty.

CIVIC RESPONSIBILITY

Vote in every election. Your vote is significant, especially at the local level. The greatest national impact is initiated locally.

Consider public service. When you serve in public office, you put yourself in an elite class of people who shape the city, state and nation.

Visit your local government buildings and get to know the workers and leaders. Volunteer at events to build relationships.

Attend council meetings. Get to know the process so that you are successful in using it.

Understand rhetoric. Become a keen listener who can dissect political statements to find fundamental truth.

Learn to communicate in a calm manner. When you address an official, be calm no matter how upsetting your concern. Your composure allows the opportunity to advance the conversation.

Become a campaign volunteer at least once. This is an inspiring way to get connected to the political process. It may even inspire you to run for office.

Be proactive to get things done in your schools and neighborhood. Be knowledgeable about what functions each city agency performs. Then, you will know who to contact for pothole repairs, crosswalks, and signal lights.

Pay attention to those who genuinely praise you. They are most likely the caliber of people who would lend support when you run for office.

SURVEY YOUR SKILLS

Write down everything that you are capable of doing. Then, prioritize your list based upon the things that have a one or two-step process. This means that after you perform step one, you get paid at step two. Promote things on your list that pay more for a few more steps. You will often be surprised by the things that emerge. Trust the process.

Take on the jobs and services that you can do alone. When it comes to getting the job done, you are the most reliable person you know. You will not have to rely on anyone else for quality or deadlines.

Try these levels of priority:

1. Do it now (Goals and Auto-imperatives).
2. Do it next (Goals and Desires).
3. Do it of necessity (Important things that come up).
4. Never do it (Things that waste your time).

Know what you are about on a deeper level. Have a full understanding of your work ethic, values and boundaries.

1. Know what you will do.
2. Know the reasons for which you apply yourself.
3. Know assuredly what you are not willing to do.
4. Know that you do not always have to give an explanation for your boundaries.

Enhance your skills to increase your value. Never be ashamed of your premium rates. Consumers recognize value and appreciate quality for the price.

STATIONS IN LIFE

Your main goal in life is to improve yourself. While others may be satisfied with where they are right now, you must constantly pursue a higher standard of living. As you do this, your reflections will always be from a superior vantage point.

You will encounter those who have far less than you. Be grateful for what you have and courteous to those who are less fortunate. Avoid the compulsion to brag or highlight your possessions. That is an indication of insecurity and insensitivity.

Do not be intimidated by those who are more fortunate than you. Take advantage of your proximity and you too will become more prosperous.

Money does not buy character. You must choose to live with character, no matter how prosperous or wealthy you become.

Build and maintain relationships with high achievers. This will inform your thinking and cause you to reach for higher goals.

You will rarely achieve anything in partnership with those who have never accomplished anything. It is permissible to like people but do not allow that to influence your judgement on productivity.

Base levels of society should remind you of your humble beginnings and heighten your resolve for success.

FAITH

Faith is the embracing of your convictions through an unknown span of time. Your faith is engaged every time you pursue something. Keep it engaged until you have what you seek.

God is faithful. God is the most reliable entity in your life. All others will fail.

Your faith is very similar to manhood in that it relies upon your determination to show up in times of difficulty.

Employ faith when embarking on new adventures.

God is our provider. He makes provisions for the just and unjust but he honors the faithful.

Faith could mean believing when nobody else does. You must trust your own judgement.

Faith can be developed just like other muscles. Give yourself repeat opportunities to bestow confidence in someone or something.

I pray that your faith increases as does your experience with God.

HONESTY

It is difficult to be honest with oneself because it requires the kind of character that faces consequences.

It is possible to physically grow to physical maturity while remaining emotionally adolescent. This may result from constantly running away from challenges. It is the main reason that so many adults are childish.

Face up and 'fess up. Confession is the how you get your freedom.

It is difficult to be honest when you realize that everyone around you operates on lies and deception. Be aware that liars must keep lying to maintain.

Be honest. Avoid people and situations where you cannot be forthright.

A Broken Heart

It is good to suffer a broken heart because it shows that you are capable of loving. Do not linger on the brokenness but learn from your experience. Realize your flaws and be thankful for an opportunity to grow.

Let your broken heart make you a better companion in the next relationship.

When you end a relationship, be kind and gentle, yet resolved. The hurt you feel is temporary and better than prolonged misery. Be more courageous than a procrastinator.

God does his greatest work with broken hearts. You are open and sensitive to the call of wisdom. Try not to act outside your character but quietly embrace the insight that comes to you.

Try to avoid becoming cynical. We have a tendency to project flaws and negative attributes on to new relationships because of past experiences. This is unhealthy for you and unfair to the person who is attempting to get to know you.

Always learn from a broken heart. Figure out what you like and dislike in personal interaction and learn to recognize compatibility.

A broken heart can be the impetus for a deeper spiritual connection. These are important moments where you can increase your faith and your spiritual pursuit. Take advantage of it.

I pray that you recover in a healthy way.

STRESS

Be at peace. Approach life as one who takes it easy. Most situations do not last long enough to even be considered temporary, so learn to let it go immediately.

Practice deep and controlled breathing. This will lower your stress and increase your concentration. When you focus on breathing, it will be difficult to give more attention to anything else.

Do not let thirty dollars get the best of you or bring out the worst in you. People are made up of proteins worth about thirty bucks if bottled and sold at a vitamin store.

You must rest. The more pressure you face, the more rest you need. Sleep with a blindfold, noise reduction earbuds and listen to audio books to block out everything.

Turn it off. Do not process during your down time. Put it down and pick it up when you rise again.

Your body does not have a natural defense for stress. Your worries can get the best of you. There may be times when you must stop caring to take care of yourself.

Be neutral or numb to things that are not worthy of your time. This is a useful approach. It keeps you from investing emotion in worthless things. Apathy may be necessary.

Practice letting go. You would lose your voice if you yelled at everyone you brushed against while walking through a crowd. You remain calm and keep moving without complaint. You let it go. This is what letting go should feel like in all areas of your life. Practice letting go.

Be a non-stick surface. Sticky situations can develop rapidly but you do not have to embrace any part of them. People will offend you but you do not have to take offense. Let it fall to the ground.

CONFLICT

Conflict happens within the space that two or more entities have in common while the uncommon areas remain at peace. Resolution is always found within the area of conflict. Careful and serious communication is required to find closure.

Conflict is best resolved through principled negotiation. This is where all parties get enough of what they need to be satisfied.

Principled negotiation is unsuccessful when dealing with those who have no principles. It is difficult to bargain with unscrupulous or unfair parties.

Do not entertain conflict with those with whom there is no resolution. Abandon any encounter where the level of thinking is inadequate to achieve success.

Avoid bad relationships. Identify them and evacuate quickly.

Fighting is a poor decision for many reasons.

1. You are too old to have physical altercations.
2. Fighting is a sign of unresolved childhood frustrations that have little to do with the person you are attempting to harm.
3. Fighting is a sign that you have contempt for the world.
4. Fighting indicates that you have not faced the pain of your past.
5. Fighting is displaced anxiety. You are taking it out on the wrong person.
6. Fighting is an unhealthy way to find resolution.
7. Fighting may cause a longer feud.

8. Fighting is a sign that you have low vocabulary and poor communication skills.

Seek counseling when your soul is afflicted.

You can learn people's true character by the way they handle conflict. That loving person who curses at you in crisis is not as loving as they appear to be.

Read books about conflict resolution. You may have a career that pays you to resolve corporate conflict.

BE THANKFUL

You are blessed and always have been.

You have favor with God. It comes in various forms.

You have food, clothing and shelter. Your basic needs are met. Find love and you are on top of the world.

You have life, peace, and contentment. This is more valuable than the other things you have.

Remember the blessing and how good God has been to you.

Be thankful every day. Complaining is a good indication of ungratefulness.

DECEPTION

The world tends to operate on deceptive practices as a standard. Question everything you see and hear. Most of it is rhetoric and promotional lies.

A half-truth and a non-truth are both rhetoric. The goal is to convince you without the burden of telling the truth at all.

Commercial rhetoric is meant to be misleading.

Television advertising is a great example of rhetoric. The greatest truth about most products is the part they omit.

Products in stores are put under brilliant light, mirrored glass and shiny chrome fixtures for enhanced perception. The products are not nearly as brilliant under natural light.

Almost every salesperson uses deceptive tactics. You can expect them to inflate the truth or omit the negatives. Always be calm when making purchases or pause the deal to come back later.

Deception is acceptable because everybody seems to participate in it. Although this is most common, do not conform to it.

Build a value system that avoids deceptive practices. There are many ways to prosper that have nothing to do with taking advantage of people.

People will show you just how deceptive they can be. Pay attention to their contradictions.

**After you have been kind to those with whom you are in relationship, allow them the opportunity to be kind to

you. This is not so you can keep tabs and demand reciprocity, but rather to evaluate the caliber of their friendship.

Do not deceive yourself. Accept the truth about the people around you and do not make excuses for their limitations.

Deceivers can teach you a lot about deception. Pay careful attention to those who attempt to take advantage of you. Listen and learn the language they use. Watch their eyes, hand gestures and body language.

People play the victim because it helps you to feel better about yourself when you help them.

When you aid deceptive people, they gain more confidence. You ultimately hurt others by helping them.

KEEP A JOURNAL

Journaling is a great way to document the seasons of your life.

Keep a different journal for various aspects of your life.

1. Have an update journal that you use about four or five times per year.
2. Record prayers, blessings, and accomplished goals.
3. Journal daily life if you are really into journaling.
4. Write letters to your children as a complete journal.
5. Have a journal for concepts and ideas.
6. Journal your innermost thoughts and concerns.
7. Journal about problems that emerge without warning.
8. Journal all the joys in your life.

Make a list of those people who influence you in significant ways. It will always be longer than the list of pain and trials you had to endure.

Journaling turns into best-selling novels. Write with a sense of knowing that your thoughts are worth money. When you publish interesting material, people will be engaged and embrace your work.

TELL YOUR STORY

Capture your thoughts on paper.

Be courageous to tell your story.

Do not hold things inside. Speak it. Write it. Film it. Publish it and release it in movie theaters.

Seek counseling. Tell your story to a professional who can help you. Be open and get to the bottom of your issue.

Publish your story. Be a legacy to others by sharing your deepest thoughts and experiences. Help others connect with their feelings by relating to yours.

Get a literary agent to manage your book career.

Write down your visions so that others see your innovation and even expound upon it.

Write method books that help others gain knowledge from using your process.

Write how-to books that save time, money and headaches for your readers.

GET SERIOUS

There are parts of your day that you must focus on the important things. This takes a great deal of seriousness. Get serious.

You must avoid playfulness at inappropriate times. People have difficulty taking you seriously when you play too much.

Learn to shift from fun mode to work mode quickly.

Plan your day. Plan your week, your month, and year.

Make plans for your life.

Execute your plan.

Get serious about your education and advancement. As an undergrad, your purpose is to graduate. As a graduate, your goal is to get an advanced degree that significantly increases your income.

Get a doctorate when you have mastered your field.

Beware

As a young man, you will be attracted to adventure and risk-taking. Beware! Some risks could cost you your life.

Do not allow anyone to convince you to take unnecessary risks for the sake of entertainment.

When it comes to life and death, there are very few do-overs.

When you are in the company of those who commit crimes, you are also guilty of their crime. You will face the same punishment for their actions. Stay away from life-long criminals and those who have no conscience. Value your freedom and respect the property of others.

You do not need a lot of friends even though you may want them. Connect with decent people and leave the rest alone. You can be jovial and then be gone.

Criminals see everyone as either a victim or an accomplice. If you are an accomplice, you will eventually become a victim. Do not run with criminals. There is a high probability that you will be arrested for the crimes they commit.

When you put yourself in the company of criminals, they will conspire to blame you when they get caught. People will say and do anything to go free.

Consider the contradiction in the phrase "snitches get stitches." When a person is free to give information, he is considered a snitch, but one who gives information while incarcerated is considered an informant. A snitch who receives money for information is a paid informant while one who calls a hotline is considered a tipster.

Every person becomes a snitch when incarcerated or compensated with money or leniency.

Stay away from predators or you may be compelled to employ predatory practices.

It is best to avoid those who live below your values.

If you get into legal trouble, get a lawyer and invoke your privilege to remain silent before investigators. Let your attorney speak for you. She or he is your only advocate.

Criminal investigators have the duty of getting a confession from you. It is their job. You have the right to remain silent. Remain silent!

I pray that you never find yourself in a legal predicament where your freedom is in jeopardy. It would be heartbreaking for everyone in your life.

SELF-IMPROVEMENT

You are good at what you do. Now, do it better.

Realize the value of maintaining excellence when you achieve it.

Your personal best should be better next time. Excellence is a vast area in which to explore.

When you arrive at greatness, it is easy to rest there, especially when people applaud you. Move from one greatness to another.

There will always be a higher level. Approach every summit with grace, knowing that there is more to learn and greater to become.

Leave people behind on a regular basis. This is an important way to recognize progress because you are in the company of some who have no intentions of going any higher. You must move on to your next assignment without hesitation.

LIVE WITH LEGACY IN MIND

Think about your future. Plan for it and act on your plans, now. Set lofty goals so that your accomplishments will be great. Have a master design for your life and work to fill in every part of the picture.

Think about your children and their success. Do little things to help them, now. Write them letters before they are born. Do all that you can to position them for success. Save money and accumulate resources for their use.

Make sure that your life has been about something bigger. Choose to do things that are impactful to many.

Start a new tradition that your family will continue for generations to come. This could be anything from a Family Fashion Show to a Family Expo, where everyone has an opportunity to display their business or service. Your family will be prosperous when every member purchases goods and services from family first.

Make every effort to accomplish something profound in your lifetime. I hope that it is something for which you are remembered and highly compensated. Set your sights on goals of significance and your achievements will exceed your expectations.

Bless God's people. God will remember you with his blessings when you bless those deserving and especially those who cannot repay you.

Donate to great causes. You will join with others to accomplish things that you may not achieve on your own.

Clean Up on Aisle Five

Obey the law. Work for what you get and be content to set goals for what you want. Do not engage in unlawful activities. The consequences are great and long-lasting. Even if you get away with it, the loot does not last or satisfy your greatest need.

Weigh your decisions carefully and always consider the outcome. Weigh your decisions carefully and always consider the outcome.

I pray that you rapidly recover from your mistakes.

Some mistakes are not easily repaired. When you betray your family and friends, your relationships may be permanently altered. You will regret hasty decisions you made in moments where you lowered your standards. You will always ask, "What was I thinking?" By that time, it is too late to correct. Please, think before you act. I mean, really think. Do not be hasty.

There could be serious implications from a chance encounter with a cute girl who thought you were cute too. You could become a father from a brief encounter and be faced with the most adverse circumstances in which to raise a child. Consider your family, your future and your legacy. This entire book revolves around it.

Have the commitment to maintain your vehicle.

1. Change the oil at its required interval.
2. Rotate your tires on schedule.
3. Wash and wax your car.
4. Do the proper tune-ups.
5. Replace shocks and struts.

6. Replace lamps and bulbs.
7. Take your vehicle to the shop at the first sign of trouble, not the last sign.

Deferred maintenance could cost hundreds of dollars to fix something that would have been fifty bucks.

Even though there is no immediate crisis, you must act with the certainty that crisis is coming. Please do not face repetitive financial crises with the same broken response. That is truly irresponsible.

Remember, you do not have the latitude to make the kinds of mistakes that my generation did. Consequences are immediate and more severe for your generation. Playful threats are taken seriously and could cause you a great deal of trouble.

MANAGE THE BLESSING

Be wise with your blessings. Preserve your resources and do not squander them. There are important things to accomplish with your resources.

Never feel guilty about your blessings, just grateful.

Put yourself in the presence of those who have as much or more than you. You will not have to defend your status.

Your safest partnerships will be with those who are affluent and hold similar values.

It is my opinion that your blessings are not designed to be given away to everyone who continuously asks or begs of you. The blessing is to demonstrate to others that God can bless them as well. You are a living example.

Be blessed and stay blessed. You must work hard to preserve and increase your resources.

Please learn to say, "No." This is often the correct answer. You must deal with the pain or guilt you may feel. Just like malodorous flatulence, it will pass.

Please learn to say, "Not now." Give yourself an opportunity to think it over. You will see that problems are resolved, even when you removed yourself from the picture.

Give wisely. Give as a way of life.

Give to the bigger and broader entity.

You are not a convenience store.

Develop a family loan corporation that is available to extended family, at little or no interest. When your loved ones refuse to pay back their loans, the corporation can fail without having any impact on the welfare of your wife and children. This failure will show them that they cannot depend upon one another. They failed because of selfishness. If it succeeds, you will have built a grand legacy.

The blessing is your seed. It is for your wife, your children, and their children. Other men should have a harvest with which to bless their families.

The blessing is not for your cousin's cousin.

God loves us and has individual and corporate blessings for one and all.

I pray that your entire family is prosperous and has a heart to contribute to the world.

CONFESS

Confess your faults to God and he will forgive you.

Confess regularly.

When you get to the bottom of your issue, deal with it and change it. Confession is acknowledging your fault and positioning yourself for positive change.

You have an abundance of grace.

Get an accountability partner. Get a mentor or friend who cares and wants the best for you. Do not walk the path of integrity alone.

Make positive affirmations about yourself. You must learn to practice saying positive thing about yourself. Be mindful of your greatest attributes and say them out loud.

Learn to say:

1. I am courageous and honest.
2. I am prosperous and loyal.
3. I am caring and resilient.
4. I am godly and reverent.

Affirmation is a form of confession. Confess your gifts and abilities.

Affirm your family, friends and colleagues. You will be surprised how powerful and meaningful your words are to others.

Never reject positive affirmation. In an effort to be humble, we often reject the good things people say about us. Receive affirmation by saying, "thank you."

BE AN EDUCATOR

Aspire to teach. This is one of the most fulfilling things you can do.

Use your greatness to inspire greatness. Your heart will be filled with joy when you see the accomplishments of those you inspired.

You must learn well to teach well.

Teach to expand your ability to communicate. Teaching develops your communication skills and allows you the opportunity to examine your theories for better pedagogy.

The books you write will have more insight because of your teaching experience. Compile all your notes into a great manuscript.

Just as you learned by watching me, your children will learn from watching you. Teach them well.

The most valuable thing you can give others is knowledge. Give freely.

Pay close attention to what students choose to read. You will have a good indication of what teaching approach will be most successful.

CELEBRATE

Celebrate people who do well. Engage and encourage them.

Celebrate your employees for a job well done. People feel appreciated when you acknowledge their efforts to make your company a success. Reward them frequently.

Celebrate those who receive a job promotion. This purges jealousy from your heart even though you may be disappointed. You are also demonstrating composure and graciousness. Others may be gracious unto you upon your promotion.

Celebrate the best part of the worst people with whom you must deal. People can really get on your nerve sometimes. Learn to raise them up with honest compliments about their strengths and try not to be around when they operate in their weakness. In worst case scenarios, remain silent. There are still people who look up to you and they would be hurt if they saw you react poorly.

Celebrate your existence. You are here. You are meaningful and you count for something bigger than you know right now. Your life is ever unfolding so you cannot predict how great you will be. Expand your thinking to realize that others depend upon you. You are constantly discovering the reason that you are here.

Celebrate your birthday in grand fashion. Be the biggest birthday boy ever. You can return to a person of humility tomorrow. It is your day and you should mark the moment with class.

Celebrate the faithfulness and loyal devotion of your wife. Spend money and lavish her with gifts. Be creative in the ways you communicate gratitude.

Celebrate your children simply because they are yours.

Celebrate holidays and holy days. Take time to observe holidays appropriately. Show respect for country and reverence for God.

Celebrate your friends. Show gratitude to your friends for their faithfulness.

Celebrate your extended-family members. Embrace your extended family for the value they bring. Make sure they realize how much you appreciate their positive contribution to your family.

Celebrate God's faithfulness. Demonstrate your gratitude and reverence for God's love and blessings upon you. Your family will embrace your gratitude and be grateful as well.

Celebrate your family for who they are, not just for what they do. Make sure that your family comprehends your love just because they are yours. Celebrate them as much as you celebrate their accomplishments. Be lavish and grand with your family.

Celebrate your favorite team. Throw watch parties so you can be loud and crazy with friends. The laughter and social encounter will be good for you, especially when your team is winning.

Celebrate for the sake of celebration. Throw yourself a party simply because the opportunity is available. Celebrate milestones, boulders, pebbles, and even grains of sand. Celebrate and gather with your friends.

Learn how to have a good time. Make yourself comfortable in each environment by engaging the liveliest group. Introduce yourself and enjoy being the odd man in the bunch. Be positive and make the best of every situation with humor.

My Prayer for You

Bless my son indeed. I pray that you are blessed in visible, tangible ways, so that your unmerited favor is undeniable. I pray that you cherish, protect, and preserve your blessings.

Bless my son in transit. I pray that you are granted safe passage in all your travels and that no harm befalls you or your traveling companions.

Grow in wisdom and discernment. I pray that you seek knowledge and use your understanding to make the right decisions in every situation you encounter. I pray that you gain the ability to employ your senses with speed and accuracy as you make decisions.

I pray the blessing of academic success. I pray that you are focused and committed to excel in every academic pursuit. I pray that you emerge within the top ranking of your class and your education advances you professionally and financially.

I pray for your financial success. I pray that you increase your money management skills. I pray that you are well compensated so that there is more than enough to both enjoy and take care of responsibilities. I pray that you can afford to travel, enjoy leisure activities and own a second home. I pray that you have a healthy work life and an amazing retirement. I pray that you leave a financial legacy for your children and their children.

I pray for protection from hurt, harm, and danger. I pray that you are never set upon by thieves. I pray that you are never injured in an automobile or industrial accident.

I pray that you meet the love of your life who finds the love of her life in you. I pray that you love with all your heart and remain faithful. I pray that you are deeply loved and respected.

I pray for the health and welfare of your marriage and that you have longevity. I pray that your family is increased and your descendants are blessed because of your love.

I pray that you have drawn positive conclusions from our time together as father and son, so that you will be a great blessing to your sons and daughters. I pray that you continue in the best examples that I set for you and that you avoid the worst of them.

I pray for your wife and children's health and that you also prosper and be in good health. As I pray for your family, you pray for them also. Pray that they remain healthy. May the Lord God sustain you.

I pray that you and your family are safe from robbers, thieves, and predators of every kind.

I pray that you find time to enjoy simple pleasures.

I pray that you enjoy time spent with your children. Take advantage of the opportunity to spend time with them while they are young. Remember, they will grow up and move on just as you did. Before long, you will be praying for your grandchildren.

I pray for the day when you can seat three generations around your table and offer prayers and blessings.

I pray that you set aside regular time with your wife and draw closer through the years.

I pray that these words of wisdom reverberate in your heart and mind and that its impact exceeds my highest expectations for you and your family.

EPILOGUE

I have come to have a great deal of concern for young men who have suffered at the hands of their fathers. The adverse effects are evident, whether it be because of his absence or a father's misguided presence. The voice of a loving father is so innately powerful that every man must live with desolation in his soul when that voice is missing. Because I have wandered through the desert of my own heart and found an oasis, I will use my voice to guide others to fresh water.

My sensitivity comes from having lived with a father who had little concern for his family. Just beyond the public façade was a home filled with his brutal physical and psychological abuse. I had no idea that I would carry the emotional damage always. As a matter of fact, the area of depredation was so vast that it would take many years before the full extent of damage was comprehended.

After forty-six years, it became clear. My mother attempted to love a man who did not have to capacity to love her. Although this fact was heartbreaking (for her), it was more devastating for her children. We suffered greatly from her decision to keep us in an unhealthy environment. The injuries he caused will stay with us for a lifetime. At present, my mother is deceased, my father, estranged, and my siblings are disconnected.

If you want to know more about my family's story, it is available in an audiobook entitled, *Turn on The Light.*

ABOUT THE AUTHOR

Eric lives in Dallas, Texas where he worked as a counselor for suicide and crisis hotlines and served 25 years in church work. He is committed to enhancing the lives of those on their journey to manhood and men who had a poor relationship with their fathers.

Eric Willis addresses a wide variety of topics that boys and young men will assuredly face in their lifetime. He provides counsel and philosophical approaches to assist them with their thinking, planning and their actions. He also discusses circumstances that sons should avoid and offers thoughtful guidance on how to navigate around trouble.

This book started as a journal written through Eric's desire to improve his son's understanding. He expounded on a list of concerns that he wanted him to consider. The words are deeply personal and everyone who reads it will realize the value of having and sharing this book. Because Eric was a single dad for several years it heightened his devotion to the task of parenting and increased his awareness of the challenges that sons face in every season of their development.

Other books:
Turn on the Light: Exposing Abuse without Confronting the Abuser (audiobook)
Handle Your Business: Music Publisher
Piano Quick
Encounters with the Word